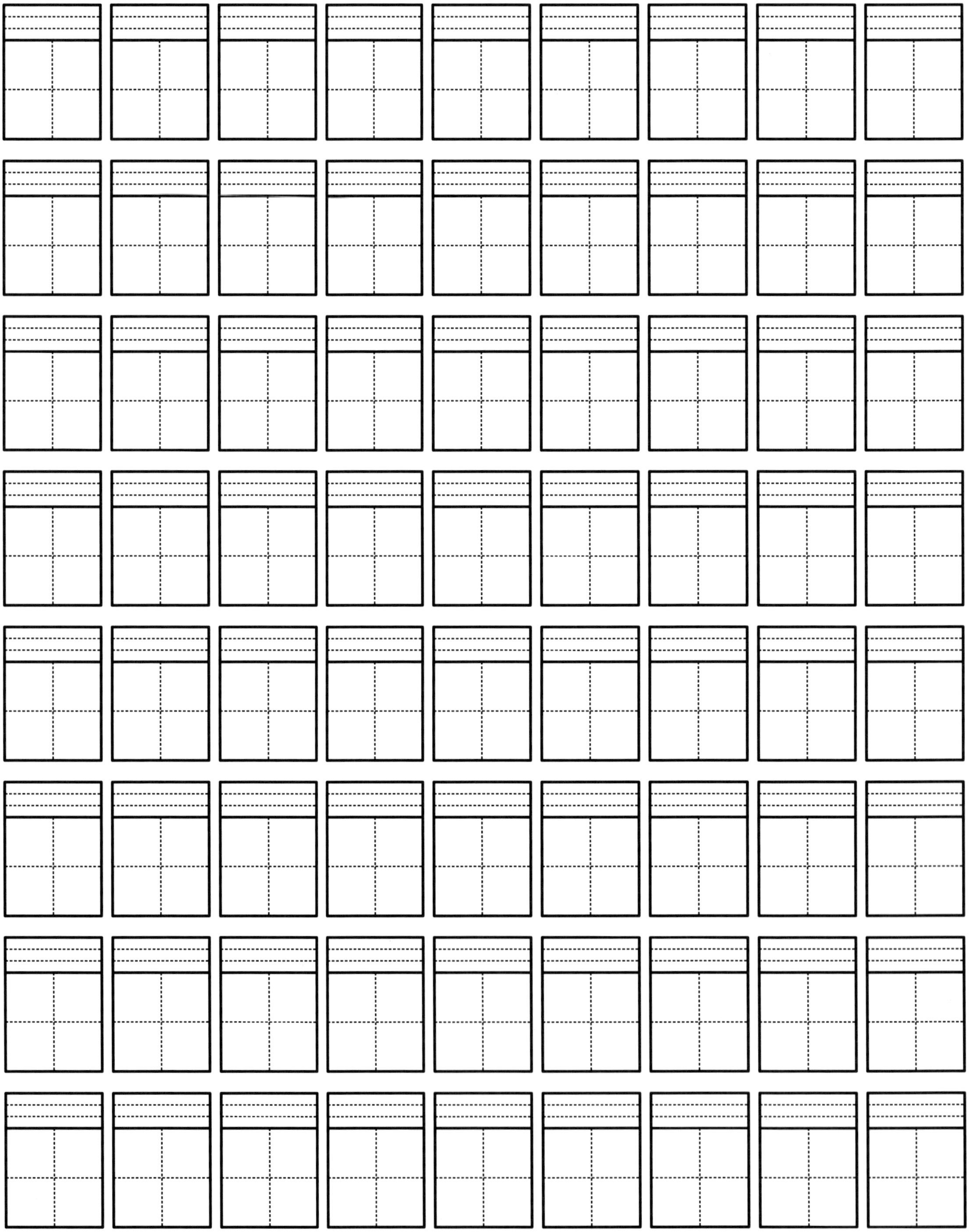

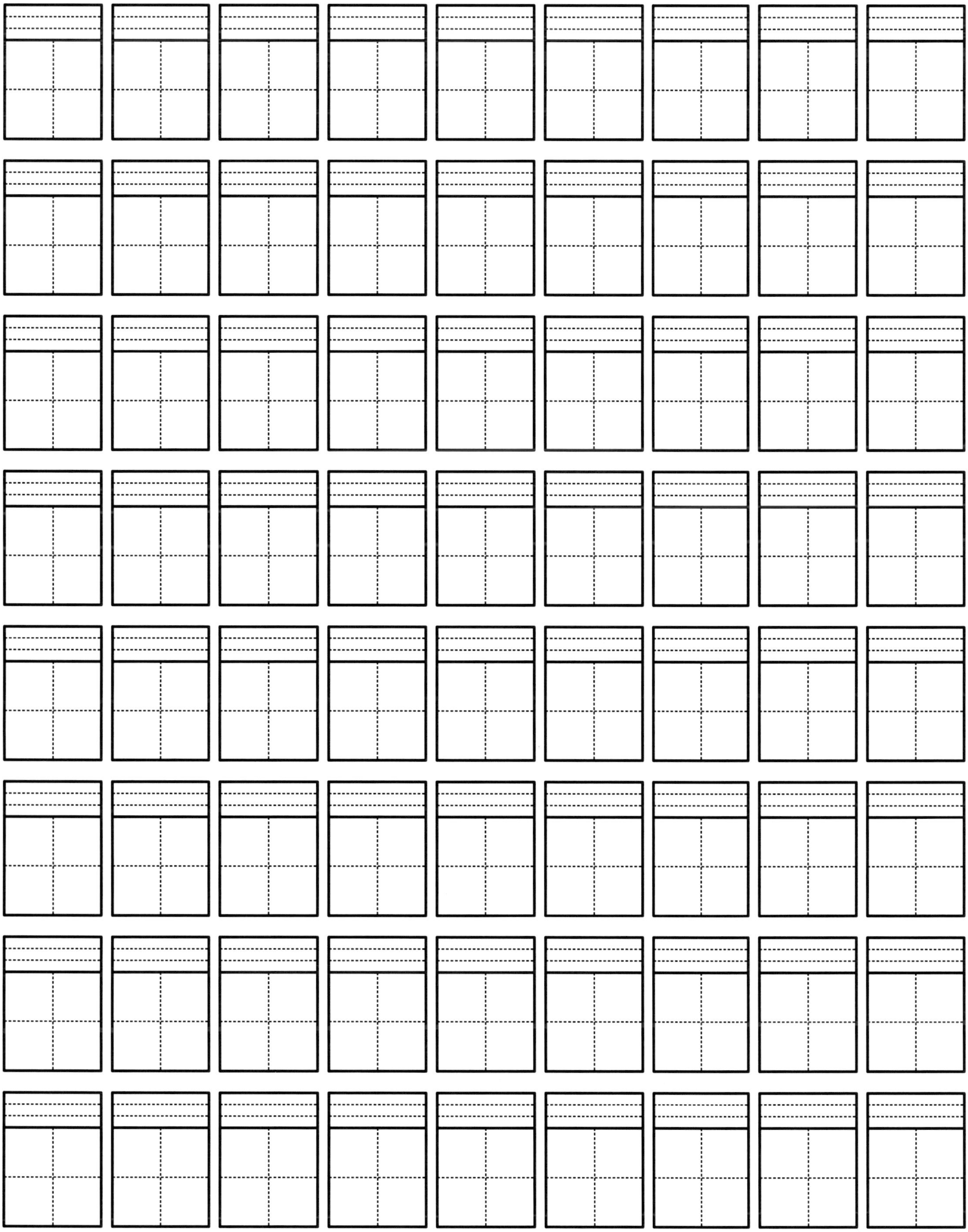

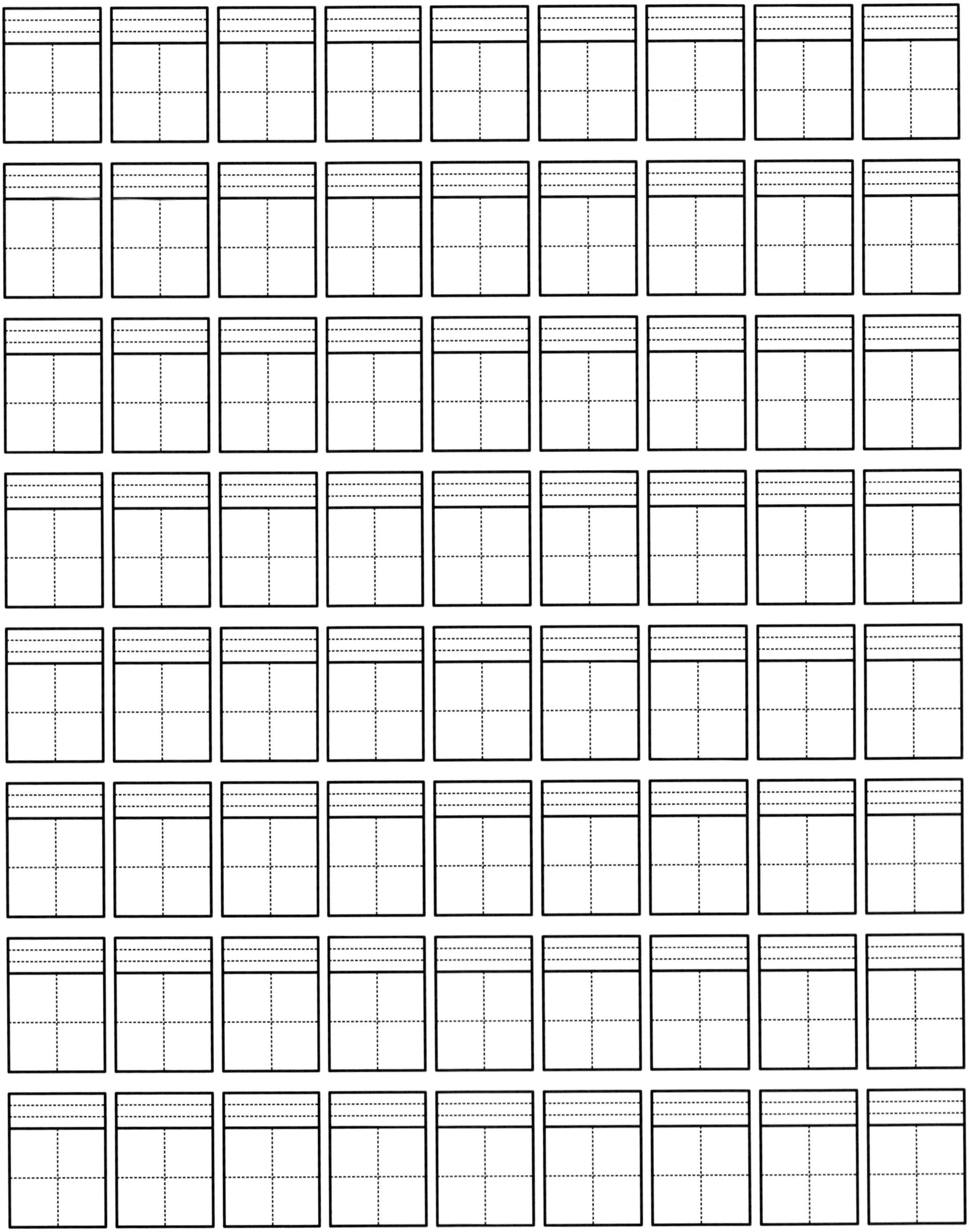

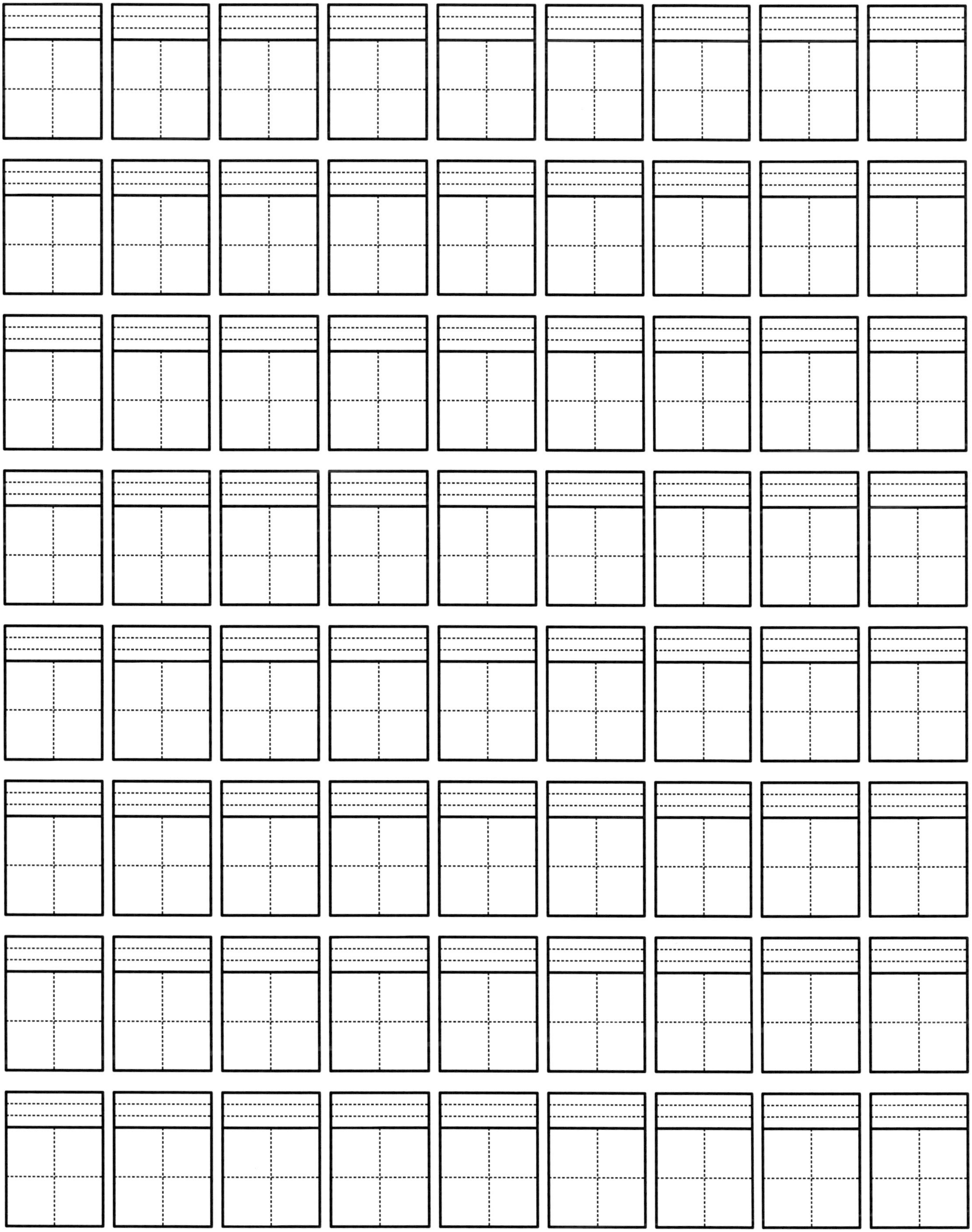

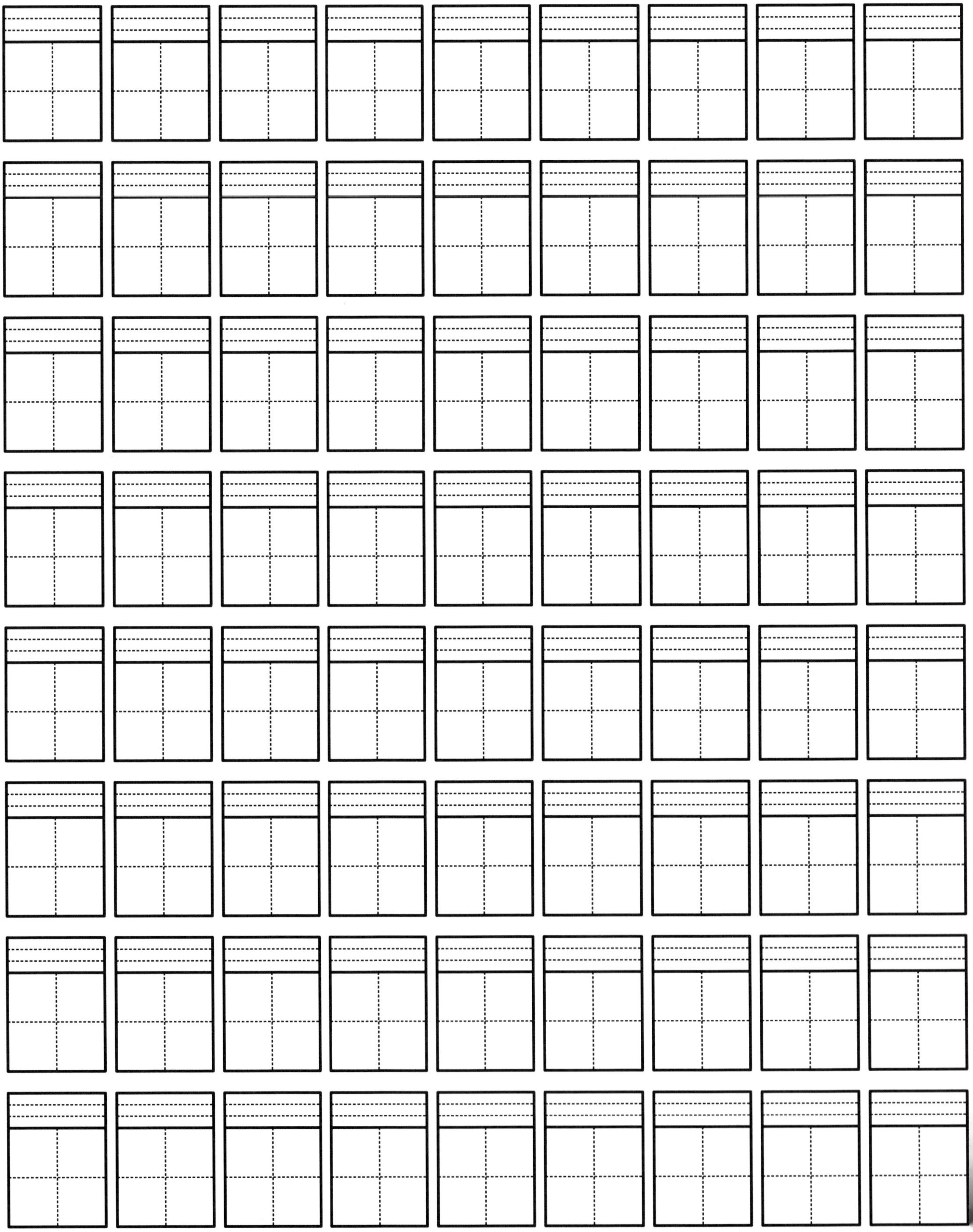

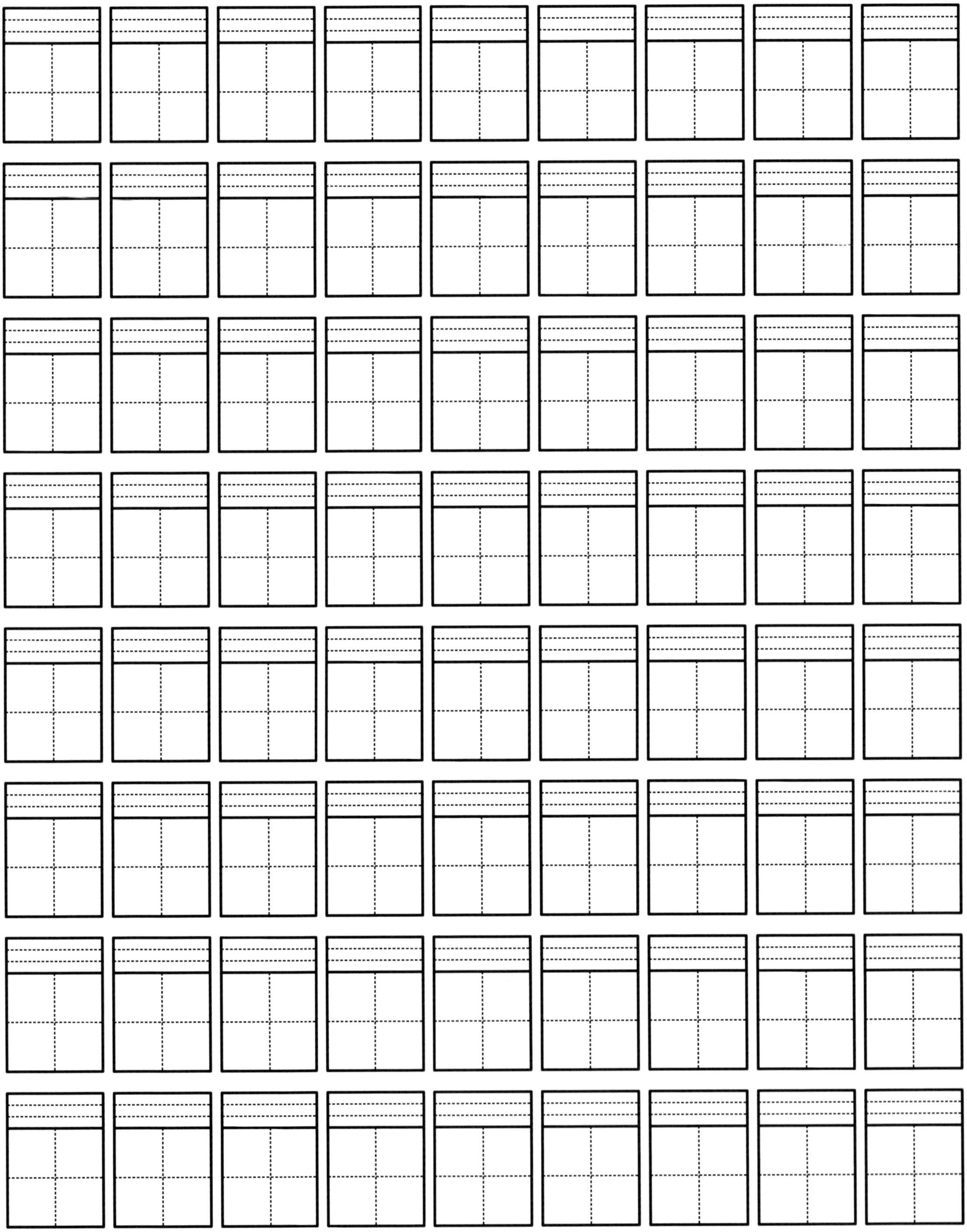

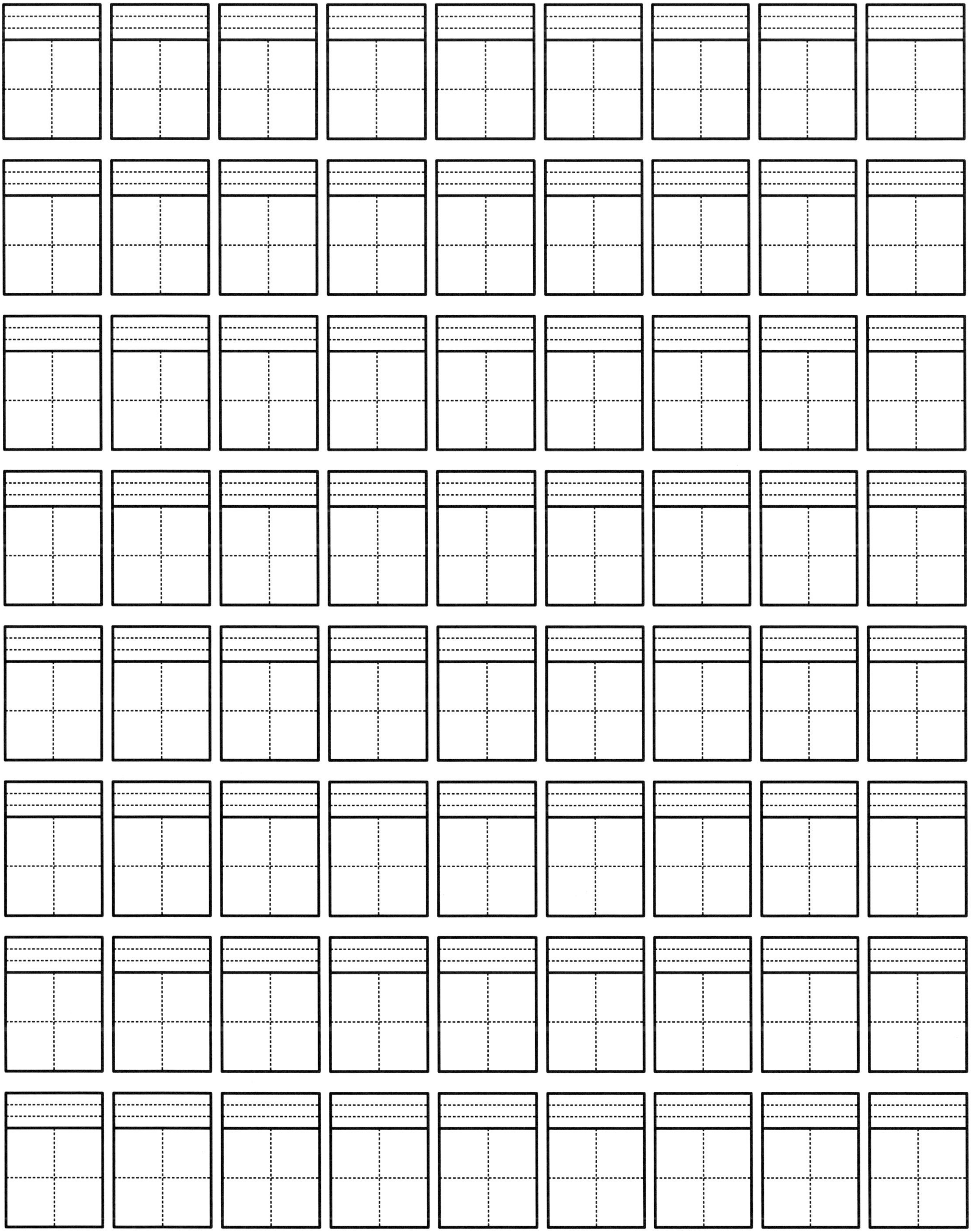

Made in United States
North Haven, CT
11 September 2023

41416446R00061